"THE
CUSTOMER
EXPERIENCE
QUOTE BOOK"

JAMES DODKINS

DEDICATION

Dedicated to CTRL+C and CTRL+V without whom this book would not have been possible.

PERSON WHO COPIED & PASTED THE QUOTES
↓

A NOTE FROM THE ~~AUTHOR~~

This is a book of Customer Experience quotes, nothing more, nothing less. I've made sure to include 365 of them so that maybe you can look at one every day, or tweet one every day or send one out to your team or write it on a notice board...I don't know, I've done the hard bit, you figure out the rest.

1

"Get closer than ever to your customers. So close that you tell them what they need well before they realize it themselves."
– Steve Jobs

2

"Your most unhappy customers are your greatest source of learning."
– Bill Gates

3

"It's easier to love a brand when the brand loves you back."
– Seth Godin

4

"Customer Experience is not a problem to be solved, but a promise to be realized."
– Steve Towers

5

"The research suggests that when we ask customers what they think and then we take no action, it yields an increased negative sentiment towards the company than if we hadn't asked at all."
– Nicolle Paradise

6

"Customer service is the experience we deliver
to our customer. It's the promise we keep to the
customer. It's how we follow through for the
customer. It's how we make them feel when
they do business with us."
– **Shep Hyken**

"Good customer experience costs less than bad customer experience."
– James Dodkins

8

"Make the customer the hero of your story."
– Ann Handley

9

"Every contact we have with a customer influences whether or not they'll come back. We have to be great every time or we'll lose them."
– Kevin Stirtz

10

"Silent customers can be deadly. Encourage them to complain."
– Ron Kaufman

11

"In the world of Internet Customer Service, it's important to remember your competitor is only one mouse click away."
– Doug Warner

12

"100% of customers are people. 100% of employees are people. If you don't understand people, you don't understand business."
– Simon Sinek

13

"To provide good customer experience, enable your employees to be real."
— **Jeanne Bliss**

14

"You can't transform something you don't understand."
– **Annette Franz**

15

"From the frontline to the executive boardroom, everyone in the company impacts the customer experience, either directly or indirectly."
– Doug Bell

16

"CX is not about creating pretty pictures. It is about adopting and embedding an approach to continuously managing the customer journey"
– Ian Golding

"At the end of the day, Customer Experience is simply people working to make other people's lives better and easier."
– Nate Brown

18

"Customers don't expect you to be perfect. They do expect you to fix things when they go wrong."
– Donald Porter

19

"So, get to know your customers. Humanize them. Humanize yourself. It's worth it."
– **Kristin Smaby**

"Loyal customers, they don't just come back,
they don't simply recommend you, they insist
that their friends do business with you."
– Chip Bell

"We see our customers as invited guests to a party, and we are the hosts. It's our job every day to make every important aspect of the customer experience a little bit better."
– Jeff Bezos

"Every great business is built on friendship."
– **J.C. Penney**

"The first step in exceeding your customer's expectations is to know those expectations."
– Roy H. Williams

24

"Customers are more likely to believe what their friends say about your company than what your marketing department does."
— **James Dodkins**

25

"When people call our call center, our reps
don't have scripts, and they don't try to up–sell.
They are just judged on whether they go above
and beyond for the customer and really deliver
a kind of personal service and emotional
connection with our customers."
– **Tony Hsieh**

"Customer service is the new marketing."
– Derek Sivers

27

"Getting service right is more than just a nice to do; it's a must do."
– **Jim Bush**

28

"If you make customers unhappy in the physical world, they might each tell 6 friends. If you make customers unhappy on the Internet, they can each tell 6,000 friends."
– Jeff Bezos

"It takes 20 years to build a reputation and five minutes to ruin it. If you think about that, you'll do things differently."
– **Warren Buffett**

"There is only one boss. The customer."
– Sam Walton

31

"Customer service is part of a holistic customer experience that is capable of providing a critical competitive advantage in today's increasingly cluttered and commoditized marketplace."
– Joseph Jaffe

32

"In the social media and online reviews era, customer service is now a spectator sport."
– Jay Baer

"Exceptional customer service is always voluntary. You can't force an employee to provide exceptional customer service any more than you can force a customer to be loyal."

– Steve Curtin

"Some people say, 'Give the customers what they want.' But that's not my approach. Our job is to figure out what they're going to want before they do."
– **Steve Jobs**

"Repeat business or behavior can be bribed.
Loyalty has to be earned."
– Janet Robinson

"The best way to find yourself is to lose yourself in the service of others."
– **Mahatma Gandhi**

37

"Many of the innovative companies got their best product ideas from customers. That comes from listening, intently and regularly."
– Tom Peters

"Here is a simple but powerful rule: always give people more than what they expect to get."
– Nelson Boswell

39

"It is not the employer who pays the wages. Employers only handle the money. It is the customer who pays the wages."
– Henry Ford

40

"Customers need E.P.I.C. service. So make it Easy, Personal & Contextual, with the customer always in Control."
– Alex Mead

"When the customer comes first, the customer will last."
– Robert Half

42

"Customer service starts where customer experience fails."
– Chris Zane

"Don't measure *if* a customer would recommend you, measure the performance that would guarantee it."
– **James Dodkins**

44

"Listen to customers and you will hear them.
Look carefully at customers and you will see
them. Do both and you will understand them."
– Ron Kaufman

"If you're not serving the customer, your job is to be serving someone who is."
– **Jan Carlzon**

"The future of communicating with customers rests in engaging with them through every possible channel: phone, email, chat, web, and social networks. Customers are discussing a company's products and brand in real time. Companies need to join the conversation."
– Marc Benioff

"You've got to start with the customer experience and work back toward the technology, not the other way around."
– Steve Jobs

"Stirring the pot is what makes innovation happen, It's what makes business go to the next level."
– Doug Bell

"I think it's very important to have a feedback loop, where you're constantly thinking about what you've done and how you could be doing it better."
– **Elon Musk**

50

"You can't expect your employees to exceed the expectations of your customers if you don't exceed your employee's expectation of management."
– Howard Schultz

"Every company's greatest assets are its customers, because without customers there is no company."
– Michael LeBoeuf

"It is so much easier to be nice, to be respectful, to put yourself in your customer's shoes and try to understand how you might help them before they ask for help, than it is to try to mend a broken customer relationship."
– **Mark Cuban**

"At the times your customers are most insecure (because service is not turning out as they expected) is the time your frontline needs to be most calm, confident and competent."

– Chip Bell

"When it comes to customer experience, If
you're not predictive in nature, great reports are
a brilliantly insightful autopsy."
– Roland Naidoo

"One of the greatest gifts you can give to anyone is the gift of attention."
– **Jim Rohn**

56

"Customers do not think in terms of sales,
marketing, operations, customer service & IT
departments. They think only of your brand. So
stop working in silos, passing the buck, and
start owning their experiences. Join everything
and everybody up, putting customers right at
the heart of your processes, always challenging
'Does this work for them?'"
– Alex Mead

"When dealing with people, remember you are not dealing with creatures of logic, but creatures of emotion."
– Dale Carnegie

58

"If you don't care, your customer never will."
– Marlene Blaszczyk

59

"Don't find customers for your products, find products for your customers."
– Seth Godin

"Open, honest communication is the best foundation for any relationship, but remember that at the end of the day it's not what you say or what you do, but how you make people feel that matters the most."

– Tony Hsieh

"People don't care how much you know until they know how much you care."
– **Theodore Roosevelt**

"We have to get more scientific about the Customer Experience."
– Steve Towers

"The drive to serve your customers consistently and meeting their ever–changing expectations with rapid innovations will always be an extra mile to achieve a never–changing loyalty."
– Ali Malik

64

"You can market all you like, but people believe what they experience."
– **Jack Mackey**

65

"The more you engage with customers the clearer things become and the easier it is to determine what you should be doing."
– **John Russell**

"If we consistently exceed the expectations of employees, they will consistently exceed the expectations of our customers."
– **Shep Hyken**

"The key is to set realistic customer expectations, and then not to just meet them, but to exceed them – preferably in unexpected and helpful ways."
– Richard Branson

"Make a customer, not a sale."
– Katherine Barchetti

69

"When it comes to innovating the customer experience, if no one is criticising you, you're doing something wrong."
– James Dodkins

"Any customer that walks away, disrespected and defeated, represents tens of thousands of dollars out the door, in addition to the failure of a promise the brand made in the first place. You can't see it but it's happening, daily."
– Seth Godin

71

"Always keep in mind the old retail adage: Customers remember the service a lot longer than they remember the price."
– Lauren Freedman

"Spend a lot of time talking to customers face to face. You'd be amazed how many companies don't listen to their customers."
– Ross Perot

73

"Our greatest asset is the customer! Treat each customer as if they are the only one!"
– Laurice Leitao

"If you don't have a fully developed complaints strategy, then all you're seeing are the snowflakes on the iceberg."
– **David Lever**

75

"The customer's perception is your reality."
– Kate Zabriskie

"It is so important to think about the way customers feel when we serve them, rather than solely focusing on the outcome we've provided"
– Alex Mead

"A customer is the most important visitor on our premises, he is not dependent on us. We are dependent on him. He is not an interruption in our work. He is the purpose of it. He is not an outsider in our business. He is part of it. We are not doing him a favor by serving him. He is doing us a favor by giving us an opportunity to do so."

– Mahatma Gandhi

"Customer service represents the heart of a brand in the hearts of its customers"
– Kate Nasser

"Every employee can affect your company's brand, not just the front–line employees that are paid to talk to your customers."
– Tony Hsieh

"Customers often know more about your products than you do. Use them as a source of inspiration and ideas for product development."
– David J. Greer

"For customer–centric organizations, experience is more than a business discipline; it is a way of life."
– Adam Toporek

"Our philosophy is that we care about people first."
– Mark Zuckerberg

"The most important thing in communication is hearing what isn't said."
– **Peter Drucker**

"Make your product easier to buy than your competition, or you will find your customers buying from them, not you."
– **Mark Cuban**

"If you make a sale, you can make a living. If you make an investment of time and good service in a customer, you can make a fortune."
– Jim Rohn

"The easiest and most powerful way to increase customer loyalty is really very simple. Make your customers happy."
– Kevin Stirtz

"We have entered the era of the customer. Today, providing customers with outstanding customer service is essential to building loyal customers and a long lasting brand."

– Jerry Gregoire

"When you learn to recognize the individual purposes of your customers, you will be able to serve them on the way they want to be served."
– Michel Falcon

89

"For us, our most important stakeholder is not our stockholders, it is our customers. We're in business to serve the needs and desires of our core customer base."
– **John Mackey**

90

"Courteous treatment will make a customer a walking advertisement."
– **J.C. Penny**

"Customers and employees – we want the same things. We want someone to know us, know our history, we want someone to listen, not interrupt us and we want some form of resolution to the things we raise."
– **Nicolle Paradise**

92

"Everything starts with the customer"
– Louis XIV

"Thinking that more KPIs will help you improve your Customer Experience is like thinking that measuring your height more often will help you grow taller."
– **James Dodkins**

"To succeed in business you need to be original, but you also need to understand what your customers want."
– Richard Branson

95

"Know what your customers want most and what your company does best. Focus on where those two meet."
– Kevin Stirtz

"As you've noticed, people don't want to be sold. What people do want is news and information about the things they care about."
– **Larry Weber**

"Building a good customer experience does not happen by accident. It happens by design."
– **Clare Muscutt**

"You never get a second chance to make a first impression."
– Will Rogers

"The way to a customer's heart is much more than a loyalty program. Making customer evangelists is about creating experiences worth talking about."
– Valeria Maltoni

100

"Businesses often forget about the culture, and ultimately, they suffer for it because you can't deliver good service from unhappy employees."
– Tony Hsieh

"When a customer complains, he is doing you a special favor; he is giving you another chance to serve him to his satisfaction. You will appreciate the importance of this opportunity when you consider that the customer's alternative option was to desert you for a competitor."
– Seymour Fine

"At stake – in every interaction – is future revenue, profitability and customer loyalty."
– Doug Bell

103

"We must answer customers in the places they prefer, not just the places our company prefers."
– **Jay Baer**

"It's one thing to sell a product to a customer. It's an entirely different thing to anticipate the needs of the customer and tell them everything they will need in order to do the job right."
– Jeremy Watkin

"Worry about being better; bigger will take care of itself. Think one customer at a time and take care of each one the best you can."
– **Gary Comer**

"Most of all, I discovered that in order to succeed with a product you must truly get to know your customers and build something for them."

– Marc Benioff

"Customers want their problem solved and day–to–day needs met. Being delighted does not meet those needs. Be consistent instead."
– Debbie Szumylo

"Customer satisfaction is worthless. Customer loyalty is priceless."
– Jeffrey Gitomer

"You have to be no less than a customer concierge, doing everything you can to make every one of your customers feel acknowledged, appreciated, and heard."
– Gary Vaynerchuk

"If you want to put your customers first, you need to put your employees first, first."
– **James Dodkins**

"CX should be leading the charge to drop the silos and work cross–functionally to serve customers better."
– Jeannie Walters

"When customers entrust you with their business, take that responsibility seriously. Listen to them, keep them informed, and own up when things go wrong. Demonstrate how valuable they are with each interaction."
– Erica Marois

"Customers see your business from a different view – their ideas may be well worth implementing."
– Marsha Collier

"Doing CX might well be the nice thing to do for the customer, but it's the *right* thing to do for your business: it delivers a faster and more sustainable growth than any other business strategy out there."
– Gustavo Imhof

"Don't do things the way they've always been done. Don't try to fit into the system. If you do what's expected of you, you'll never accomplish more than others expect."
– Howard Schultz

"Every day we're saying, 'How can we keep this customer happy?' How can we get ahead in innovation by doing this, because if we don't, somebody else will."
– Bill Gates

"Harnessing feedback and ideas to improve your customer experience should be the priority of any business."
– Mitch Belsley

"Outlove your competition."
– Seth Godin

"Zappos is a customer service company that just happens to sell shoes."
– **Tony Hsieh**

120

"I've never gone into business to make money. Every Virgin product and service has been made into a reality to make a positive difference in people's lives. And by focusing on the happiness of our customers, we have been able to build a successful group of companies."
– **Richard Branson**

"Every interaction you have with another person (whether customer, employee, friend, or family member) makes a bigger impact than you realize. Every single interaction matters. Every moment makes a difference."
– Donna Cutting

"There is no quicker way to let a customer know that you don't care about how they feel than forcing them to distil complex emotions down to a number on a predetermined scale."
– **James Dodkins**

"It's really hard to design products by focus groups. A lot of times, people don't know what they want until you show it to them."
– Steve Jobs

"Serving customers helps you grow. It helps you build a company that is admired in a way other companies are not."
– Michel Falcon

125

"We've had three big ideas at Amazon that we've stuck with for 18 years, and they're the reason we're successful: Put the customer first. Invent. And be patient."
– Jeff Bezos

"Customer service is what you do, customer experience is how you do it."
– **James Gilmore**

"You have to create an emotional experience that's so sticky, so engaging, so compelling that they don't want to leave."
– James Archer

"Clients want either the best or the least expensive."
– Tom Field

"Historically, our number–one growth driver has been from repeat customers and word of mouth."
– Tony Hsieh

"No response *is* a response: it's a response that says 'we care so little about your dissatisfaction that we refuse to even acknowledge it.'"
– **Jay Baer**

"Customers who are merely satisfied remain your customers only as long as everything goes their way."
– Chip Bell

"The customer is not always right. But, they are always the customer."
– **Shep Hyken**

"Businesses talk a lot about customer loyalty. It makes sense: A person you can count on to buy from you again and again is more valuable than one who disappears after the first transaction."
– **Mikkel Svane**

"The easiest customer to get is the one you already have."
– Norm Brodsky

"If you own the problem you own the customer. If you lose the problem you lose the customer."
– Robin Crow

"Great companies that build an enduring brand have an emotional relationship with customers that has no barrier. And that emotional relationship is of the most important characteristic, which is trust."
– Howard Schultz

"If leaders take care of the employees, the employees will take care of the customers and the customers will take care of the revenue."
– James Dodkins

"It is not your customers job to remember you. It is your responsibility to make sure they do not have the chance to forget you"
– Patricia Fripp

"Listen first. Don't react, don't assume, don't push the script or company line until you have fully heard the customer. You might even need to keep listening a bit more after you think you've 'heard' them to get it right."
– Jon Wolske

"Great customer experiences don't happen by accident."
– Nienke Bloem

"It's more important that we make an emotional connection with the customer."
– **Tony Hsieh**

"The emotional connection, the experience you create, how you make your customers feel is the differentiator between buying with you or not."
– Claire Boscq–Scott

"CX is 100% gut instinct and 100% science. If you trust your gut, but know the science, you'll go twice as far as anyone else."
– **Clint Payne**

"You need to stay ahead of your customers needs like they're a horror movie villain. You stand still, you die."
– Alex Hannon

"Focus on leading indicators. Survey results measure what the customer already experienced."
– Lynn Hunsaker

"Getting clarity around the big moments of truth in your customer experience is far more useful than creating a complex map of each individual touch point and possible path a customer could take."
– Doug Bell

147

"If there's one reason we have done better than of our peers in the Internet space over the last six years, it is because we have focused like a laser on customer experience."
– Jeff Bezos

148

"The reason it seems that price is all your customers care about is that you haven't given them anything else to care about."
– **Seth Godin**

"Big data and algorithms are not panacea for fixing poor customer experiences. People are not statistics and their experiences are inherently and deeply personal. To create remarkable products and services which improve people's lives, businesses have to resolve the tension between numbers and meaningful human experiences."

– Alex Genov

"Innovation needs to be part of your culture.
Customers are transforming faster than we are,
and if we don't catch up, we're in trouble."
– Ian Schafer

151

"Customer Experience Management = The art and science of coaxing lifetime loyalty from daily transactions."
– Steve Curtin

"Customer experience isn't an expense. Managing customer experience bolsters your brand."
– **Stan Phelps**

153

"The point of the story is that every single interaction, the most minute details of the interaction you have with your customer, are an opportunity for you to create something remarkable."
– Joey Coleman

154

"CX stands for constant experimentation. Keep trying. If it fails, you will learn and get data."
– Des Cahill

"There is no excuse for needless complexity. Go figure out your customers' needs and align everything to achieving them. The result is simple, swift and effective"
– Steve Towers

"The goal as a company is to have customer service that is not just the best, but legendary."
– Sam Walton

157

"Expectation gaps create negative memorability which is perhaps the worst possible scenario for both CX and branding. It's better to go small and deliver than to go big and disappoint."
– **Mary Drumond**

"Customers should be first, center and last for everything!"
– Steve Towers

"Customer experience is the new marketing battlefront."
– Chris Pemberton

160

"In addition to building better products, a more open world will also encourage businesses to engage with their customers directly and authentically."
– Mark Zuckerberg

"If you can turn your employees into fans of your customers they will turn your customers into fans of your company."
– James Dodkins

"Each business is a victim of Digital Darwinism, the evolution of consumer behavior when society and technology evolve faster than the ability to exploit it."
– **Brian Solis**

"Experience is the teacher of all things."
– **Julius Ceasar**

164

"You can't just ask customers what they want and then try to give that to them. By the time you get it built, they'll want something new."
– Steve Jobs

"Don't waste customers' time asking them questions unless you are prepared to act on what they say."
– **Bruce Temkin**

"How you treat your customers is who you are as a person."
– **Adam Toporek**

167

"Hell hath no fury like a customer scorned!"
– Dave Carroll

"The way you treat your employees is the way they will treat your customers."
– **Richard Branson**

"When a brand connects with their customer, that in some ways is the easy part, the hard part is keeping the customer at the center after the success/profits comes flooding in. Success can breed complacency, success can breed arrogance."
– Anna Farmery

"The most valuable resource you can give customers is your time. Listen to them to uncover their real needs. Only then can you find a way to solve their problems or meet their expectations. Treat the cause, not just the symptoms."
– Ginger Conlon

"You can acquire some measure of knowledge from various research techniques, but nothing beats living, breathing and feeling the same things your customers do."

– John Jantsch

"Organizations that implement learning relationships are better able to understand and anticipate a customer's unique needs. Learning organizations understand that great customer experiences start with listening to the customer to learn instead of talking to the customer to sell."

– Alan See

173

"Welcome to a new era of marketing and service in which your brand is defined by those who experience it."
– Brian Solis

"The term customer experience won't exist in the organisation of the future it will be so deeply entrenched in a company's product process and culture that it will be synonymous with the brand and represent the only way to do business"
– Ann Lewnes

"Don't try to tell the customer what he wants. If you want to be smart, be smart in the shower. Then get out, go to work, and serve the customer!"
– **Gene Buckley**

176

"Be the best part of your customer's day."
– John R. DiJulius III

177

"It is better to reach your customers' hearts than their wallets. If you can touch your customers heart, profits will follow."

– Ron Johnson

"The most important single thing is to focus obsessively on the customer. Our goal is to be earth's most customer–centric company."
– Jeff Bezos

"Your company cannot give good customer service if your employees don't feel good about coming to work."
– Martin Oliver

"Consumers live in an emotional world; their emotions influence their decisions. Great brands transcend specific product features and benefits and penetrate people's emotions."
– Leonard Berry

"One customer's bad experience can quickly become thousands of potential customer's bad first impression."
– **James Dodkins**

"Given the choice most customers seek out experiences and products that deliver more value, more connection, and more experience that changes for the better."
– Seth Godin

"People can copy your products and your services, but seldom can they build the powerful connections with customers that emerge from the well–designed experiences that you deliver"

– Joseph Michelli

184

"Make your recovery plan fool proof. Recruit people who communicate effectively, act quickly and resolve with empathy. Set some principles and bin the 'recovery' policies. Everyone will feel better."
– **Sandra Thompson**

185

"If your existing customers aren't sending new customers to you, you're doing it wrong."
– Joe Calloway

"Delivering great customer experiences is like being funny. Most people overestimate themselves on both fronts."

– Joseph Michelli

"Choose the customer over convenience."
– Donna Cutting

"Serving customers helps you grow. It helps you build a company that is admired in a way other companies are not."
– Michel Falcon

"While many of the processes and activities associated with the operational side of customer experience are undeniably important, necessary and effective, they are rarely the ideal starting point in building an effective customer experience strategy."
– **Gerry Brown**

"Innovation that matters will involve a hard look at what your customer experience is and what it could be. If your company isn't relentlessly focused on what is useful, digital Darwinism is going to leave you out on a forgotten branch of the evolutionary tree."
– Pete Sena

"Just having satisfied customers isn't good enough anymore. If you really want a booming business, you have to create raving fans."
– Ken Blanchard

192

"The sole reason we are in business is to make life less difficult for our clients."
– **Matt Odgers**

"Thank your customer for complaining and mean it. Most will never bother to complain. They'll just walk away."
– Marilyn Suttle

"My advice is to answer every customer, in every channel, every time. This is different from how most businesses interact with customers, especially online, which is to answer some complaints, in some channels, some of the time."
– Jay Baer

195

"Until you understand your customers, deeply and genuinely, you cannot truly serve them."
– Rasheed Ogunlaru

"No matter where you are in the world. Customers only speak one language, it's called 'Experience'."
– James Dodkins

"A good design shows respect for your customer and you're either respectful of their time or respectful of what it is that they desire, and so it makes it a very fundamental element to everything that you do."
– **Penny Wilson**

"Google Emotional Intelligence and learn how to nurture it in your organization. Your customers will thank you for it."
– Sandra Thompson

"Companies need to treat customers the way that customers want to be treated, and so to know how that is, we need to ask."
– Nicolle Paradise

"People will sit up and take notice of you if you will sit up and take notice of what makes them sit up and take notice."
– Harry Selfridge

"The greatest ROI in customer service comes from a difficult situation prevented."
– **Adam Toporek**

202

"Everyone is not your customer."
– Seth Godin

"Most of us understand that innovation is enormously important. It's the only insurance against irrelevance. It's the only guarantee of long–term customer loyalty."
– Dr. Gary P. Hamel

"To earn the respect (and eventually love) of your customers, you first have to respect those customers."
– **Colleen Barrett**

"Customers won't care about any particular technology unless it solves a particular problem in a superior way."
– Peter Thiel

"Businesses can't afford to react to what their customers want; they need to anticipate their needs."
– Parker Harris

"Make customer relationships a shared responsibility for your entire organization."
– **Mikkel Svane**

"The feedback you get from exchanging audible words will change your product and how you run your business because you get a level of honesty that gets distilled away with short email exchanges."
– **Josh Pigford**

"Customer support is not an expense to be minimized, but an opportunity to be maximized."
– Dharmesh Shah

"Good service comes naturally from satisfied employees who embraced the company culture."
– Tony Hsieh

211

"Nothing influences people more than a recommendation from a trusted friend."
– Mark Zuckerberg

212

"The first 20 years of the web were won by those that built the best infrastructure. Now it's won by those that build the best experiences."
– Aaron Levie

"Every customer interaction is a marketing opportunity."
– Stewart Butterfield

214

"If our customers aren't successful, neither are we."
– David Nevogt

215

"Teams can only improve customer experience by focusing on metrics that track the progress of their survey results' action plans."
– Lynn Hunsaker

216

"Allow your employees the freedom and empowerment to surprise and delight people."
– **Craig McVoy**

"When you're trying to make an important decision, and you're sort of divided on the issue, ask yourself: If the customer were here, what would she say?"

– Dharmesh Shah

"The best way to acquire new customers is to make your current customers excited and happy about your products."
– Mikkel Svane

"Today successful companies start with the customer. They recognize that customers spend their time across many channels, and wherever those customers are, that's where they should be meeting their customers' needs."
– Tien Tzuo

"Take every opportunity to spend time with your customer."
– Ross Mason

"There are two essential elements for achieving customer experience employee engagement, a reason and a voice."
– Mitch Belsley

"Customer Experience should drive the technology, not be driven by it."
– **James Dodkins**

223

"A complaint is a chance to turn a customer into a lifelong friend."
– **Richard Branson**

"You'll learn more in a day talking to customers than a week of brainstorming, a month of watching competitors, or a year of market research."
— **Aaron Levie**

225

"To be a true customer–centric team or organisation, you have to be willing to put your ego to one side."
– David Cancel

"A strong understanding of the outcome customers want, and how they currently get it, is essential for you to succeed."
– **Des Traynor**

"If you're genuinely building something that is solving a problem for your customers, the only people you should care about are your customers."
– **Josh Pigford**

228

"How would your company act if every customer were your Mom?"
– Jeanne Bliss

"Thinking about your purpose is actually pretty crucial to your success as a company and a brand: Not only does it give customers something to believe in, but it will inspire your team to think bigger, and make your product better."
– Hiten Shah

"Customer relationships matter more than ever, because your future revenue depends on those relationships lasting well beyond a single transaction."
– **Mikkel Svane**

"Companies have woken up to the fact that people want outcomes, not ownership. They want customized experiences, and they want continuous improvement, not planned obsolescence."
– **Tien Tzuo**

232

"Create fewer ruined days for customers!"
– Jeannie Walters

"Fall in love with your customers."
– Lynn Hunsaker

234

"The first step to exceeding customer expectations is to know what they are. Ask them."
– Bill Quiseng

"Focusing on the customer makes a company more resilient."
– Jeff Bezos

236

"Find ways to "WOW" your customer."
– Steve Digioia

"The greatest technology in the world hasn't replaced the ultimate relationship building tool between a customer and a business; the human touch."
– **Shep Hyken**

"If you are in search of real improvement in your customer experience, don't waste your time on a project. Install a process."
– **Doug Bell**

239

"The most simple form of service personalization is to learn and use your customer's name."
– Becky Roemen

"Customer service is reactive, whereas customer experience is, by nature, proactive."
– David Reid

"The best customer service is if the customer doesn't need to call you, doesn't need to talk to you. It just works."
– Jeff Bezos

"If your work doesn't begin and end with the customer, it's time to redesign your work."
– David Porter

243

"At the heart of every amazing branding strategy is the customer and how they experience the brand."
– Mary Drumond

"You will never consistently deliver customer success until you consistently measure the things that deliver it."
– **James Dodkins**

"Be consistent. To achieve positive customer experience, consistency is the key."
– **Christa Heibel**

"Listen everywhere. Don't depend on a single channel, or a narrow slice of the internet. "
– **Sid Banerjee**

"No two customers are alike. If you treat them like they are, you will never have a People–First Culture."
— **Michel Falcon**

"CX is how you make people feel about themselves when they interact with your brand."
– **Chantel Botha**

"If you don't appreciate your customers, someone else will."
– **Jason Langella**

250

"Customers want to be 'cared for' and 'cared about!"
– **Joseph Michelli**

251

"A customer talking about their experience with you is worth ten times that which you write or say about yourself."
– David J. Greer

252

"Cultivating loyalty is a tricky business. It requires maintaining a rigorous level of consistency while constantly adding newness and a little surprise – freshening the experience without changing its core identity."
– **Micah Solomon**

253

"You are only as good as your first Moment of Truth."
– Steve Towers

"Immerse yourself in the customer's world and get to know their struggles and triumphs inside out."
– Dane Brookes

"Your front-line employees are the most untapped source of customer information in your organization."
– Daniel Toro

"Our customers are not our competitors. We compete for them, not with them."
– T Jay Taylor

"A satisfied customer is the best strategy of all."
– **Michael LeBoeuf**

"Know and understand the customer so well
the product or service fits him and sells itself."
– Peter Drucker

"Great CX will never happen when the convenience of the customer is sacrificed for the convenience of the company."
– **Gautam Mahajan**

"The customer expects you to have knowledge of their stuff, not just your stuff."
– **Jeffrey Gitomer**

"Listen to your customers, not your competitors."
– Joel Spolsky

"The simple truth is that technology is still a poor substitute for human interaction."
– **Robert G. Thompson**

"We cannot promote our brands as responsive, caring and customer–focused while ignoring too many of our customers needs and complaints in social media."
– **Augie Ray**

"Customers who love you will market for you more powerfully than you can possibly market yourself."

– Jeanne Bliss

265

"The tides of change have been working, and customers have realized they control the brand, not the company."
– **Frank Eliason**

266

"Customer Experience isn't a department, it's a culture."
– James Dodkins

267

"Customers can punish or praise companies within seconds from the palms of their hands."
– **Jay Baer**

"The rules of customer experience management haven't changed all that much. You still need to be proactive, preventative, and personal."
– John Goodman

269

"The tables have turned. Today's consumers are more empowered than ever before."
– Robert Rose

270

"Exceptional customer experiences are the only sustainable platform for competitive differentiation."
— **Kerry Bodine**

"Think of your worst customer on his or her worst day. This is when you'll really discover how to be ready for the hiccups that are bound to happen, even with your best customer."
— **Jeannie Walters**

"Your target customers have to love you more than they hate change. And people really hate change."
— **Erika Hall**

"No matter how beautiful the visual design is, if it fails to help our users achieve their goals, it's bad design."
— **Crystal C. Yan**

"Customers don't care about your policies. Find and engage the need. Tell the customer what you can do."
— **Alice Sesay Pope**

275

"Customers are no longer buying products and services – they are buying experiences delivered via the products and services."
– Gregory Yankelovich

276

"People think of loyalty as a customer for a lifetime, but it's really much simpler than that. It's about the next time, every time."
– **Shep Hyken**

"Even your most loyal customers always have a choice about where to take their business."
– **Marilyn Suttle**

"Determine what your customers need and work backward, even if it requires learning new skills. Kindle is an example of working backward."

– Jeff Bezos

"People will forget what you did, but people will never forget how you made them feel."
– Maya Angelou

280

"The customer experience is the next competitive battleground."
– **Jerry Gregoire**

"If a brand can give its customers some of their precious time back, then it will be seen as delivering value."
– **Craig McVoy**

"Customers are irrational, don't fight it, embrace it! Customers buy emotionally and justify with logic."
– Colin Shaw

"CX quality is a function of how well each brand aligns its CX vision with the needs, wants, and preferences of the particular set of customers that it chooses to serve."

– **Megan Burn**

"The term Customer Relationship Management has been around for a long, long time but is it still relevant? Do customers really want to be 'managed' in this day and age?"
– Yiannis Maos

"Revolve your world around the customer and more customers will revolve around you."
– **Heather Williams**

286

"Profit isn't the goal, amazing customer experience is. Profit is the reward."
– **James Dodkins**

"The magic formula that successful businesses have discovered is to treat customers like guests and employees like people."
– Tom Peters

"Do what you do so well that they will want to see it again and bring their friends."
– **Walt Disney**

"Loyal customers don't just come back, buy more, or recommend. They tell poignant stories on your behalf."
– Chip Bell

"When someone comes to me with a cost saving idea, I don't immediately jump up and say yes. I ask: what's the effect on the customer?"
– Herb Kelleher

"The only purpose of customer service is to change feelings."
– Seth Godin

"Ask your customers to be part of the solution, and don't view them as part of the problem."
– **Alan Weiss**

"Sometimes one can become lost in a big company and lose sight of how what one does truly helps or impacts the end customer. If you are one of those, think of a fire brigade, a line of people passing buckets of water from one to the other from a source of water to the site of the fire. An individual in the brigade may not be able to see the end result, i.e., the water being thrown on the fire to put it out, but the contribution of the individual is indispensable to the final outcome."

– Grant Bright

"The most important adage and the only adage is, the customer comes first, whatever the business, the customer comes first."
– Kerry Stokes

"How you think about your customers influences how you respond to them."
– Marilyn Suttle

"Bottom–line obsession comes from turning the pursuit of money into a God and forgetting the real master your business serves: The Customer."
— **Michael Shevack**

"You'll never have a product or price advantage again. They can be too easily duplicated. But a strong customer service culture cannot be copied."
– Jerry Fritz

298

"A brand is no longer what we tell the customer it is – it is what customers tell each other it is."
– **Scott Cook**

"Strategy is easy, culture is hard, and scale is impossible."
– Adam Toporek

"Treating customers with dignity and respect starts with treating employees the same way. In order to deliver customer dignity, employees need to feel it, experience it, and receive it themselves. And they need to be encouraged to weave the delivery of dignity into their interactions with customers. Simply, enable people to care."
– Jeanne Bliss

"Any business that truly cares about customers must allow their front line employees to express their own personalities, act naturally and spontaneously and by doing this, engage with the customer emotionally as well as practically."
– Gerry Brown

302

"Companies designed for success in the 20th century won't be successful in the 21st."
– Kevin Howard

"One customer well taken care of could be more valuable than $10,000 worth of advertising."
– **Jim Rohn**

304

"The purpose of a business is to create a customer."
– Peter Druker

"Consumers are statistics. Customers are people."
– Stanley Marcus

"Understanding what customers do allows you to predict what they will do next."
– **Colin Shaw**

"The problem many of us face is that most of our management techniques were created at a time when the two–way customer conversation didn't exist."
– Jeff Gothelf

"In Customer Experience, your first impression should leave a lasting impression."
– James Dodkins

309

"Our philosophy is about delivering happiness to our customers and employees."
– **Tony Hsieh**

"Customer feedback is cheap. Actionable insight can be valuable. Taking action on insight is precious."
– Bruce Temkin

311

"Marketing needs to know more about sales, sales needs to know more about marketing, and we all need to know more about our customers."
– Jill Rowley

"We have a trillion reasons for leaders to deploy a bit more empathy."
– **Nicolle Paradise**

313

"Left to their own devices, the one thing your customers want to avoid is change."
– Brent Adamson

"Even the most complex journeys of designing and executing greater customer experiences started with simply listening and empathizing with your customers."
– Ali Malik

"It's about caring enough to create value for customers. If you get that part right, selling is easy."
– Anthony Iannarino

"The term 'frontline' is stupid, they aren't in a war with the customers."
– **James Dodkins**

"People don't buy what you do, they buy why you do it."
– **Simon Sinek**

"The number one thing to start a customer experience movement is to give everyone a voice."

– Doug Bell

319

"That which is communicated poorly is executed disastrously."
– Adam Toporek

"If your competitors start copying you, then you are doing something right!"
– Jay Baer

"The best way to control your customer experience is to intentionally create it."
– **Elle Robertson**

322

"We take most of the money that we could have spent on paid advertising and instead put it back into the customer experience. Then we let the customers be our marketing."

– Tony Hsieh

"In a world where things increasingly become commodities (especially services) the real differentiator becomes the personal experience you are able to create in the lives of your customers."
– **John Bessant**

"Sadly, the stark truth of the matter is that very few large firms will prioritize their customers until their existence depends on becoming more customer centric."

– Robert Dew

"Customers may not know that they're providing feedback, but they're voting with their wallets."
– **Jeff Gothelf**

"Few things generate more goodwill and repeat business than being effortless to deal with."
– Matt Watkinson

"Smart companies aren't trying to pitch products to strangers anymore. They're figuring out how to grow, monetize and build an ongoing, mutually beneficial relationship with a dedicated base of subscribers."

– Tien Tzuo

"The more advocates you have, the fewer ads you have to buy."
– **Dharmesh Shah**

"Companies both large and small have been drawn to a more nimble, iterative approach to innovation and growth, but as they soon discover, doing so requires a different way of interacting with current and prospective customers."
– Eric Ries

"Being truly customer–centric means having a deep understanding of your customers' unmet needs."
– Maria Martinez

"Sell the dream, tell the story, and create the emotion that the customers will feel when they work with you."
– **Craig McVoy**

"There's no such thing as B2B companies, only B2C. Some just have more B's in between them and the C."
– James Dodkins

"We believe making customers happy is about building remarkable experiences designed to leave them with specific feelings and memories worth sharing."
– Robert Dew

"Customer experiences that eliminate confusion, uncertainty and anxiety reap the rewards, generating a competitive advantage, loyalty and a peerless brand image."
– Matt Watkinson

335

"There are many reasons why customers leave, but the main reason is that businesses systematically ignore the emotional journey of the customer."
– **Joey Coleman**

336

"Our goal is to not simply understand customer behavior, but to learn how to change customer behavior and build a sustainable business."
– **Eric Ries**

337

"If the customer experience matters so much, why is it often so poor?"
– **Matt Watkinson**

"The most powerful and enduring brands are built from the heart."
– **Howard Schultz**

"Listening to feedback makes customers feel more appreciated and part of the value creation process."
– Ray Poynter

"You need to become an acknowledged expert on the customer: their issues, pains, desires, how they think – and for business products, how they work, and how they decide to buy."
– Marty Cagan

"Fundamentally, customers do not want choice;
they just want exactly what they want."
– **B. Joseph Pine II**

342

"If you don't know your customer's expectations you do not know what you are doing."
– Steve Towers

343

"Truly listening is hearing the needs of the customer, understanding those needs and making sure the company recognizes the opportunities they present."
– Frank Eliason

"If your customers are made to feel as if they are outsiders, they will eventually find a competitor who makes them feel better about doing business with them."
– **Shep Hyken**

"Find a way to be personal with your customers and connect with them on a human level."
– **Andrew Reid**

"Fix the experience *in* the experience, don't wait for the complaint."
– James Dodkins

"It's the way that companies do business and the way their incentives and structures are set up that creates a blind spot around customer experience, and that blind spot is the problem."
– Joey Coleman

348

"If you respect the customer as a human being, and truly honor their right to be treated fairly and honestly, everything else is much easier."
– **Doug Smith**

349

"Unless you have 100% customer satisfaction,
you must improve."
– Horst Schulz

350

"Each experience we deliver has a story and every single time we interact with a customer we create a memory. We have control over the lasting memory we leave with the customer."
– Guy Farthing

"If you get everybody in the company involved in customer service, not only are they 'feeling the customer' but they're also getting a feeling for what's not working."
– Penny Handscomb

"Whoever understands the customer best, wins."
— **Mike Gospe**

353

"The single most important thing to remember about any enterprise is that there are no results inside its walls. The result of a business is a satisfied customer."
– Peter Drucker

"There are only two types of companies. Ones who have customers that love them and ones who don't."
– **James Dodkins**

"People want to spend time doing the things they love, with those they love being with. If you're a brand whose product is an experience, make it more enjoyable than any other. If you're brand sells a product that customers must have, make it as easy as possible to get it out of the way. No one ever said "I can't wait for my car insurance renewal."
– Craig McVoy

356

"We are people who care about people. Our vision is simple. We care for our customers and their customers."
– Adrienne Paskell

"Many companies talk nonchalantly about excellence as if it were something they could bestow on themselves. The best, and in fact the only, arbiters of excellence are customers."
– **Gerry Brown**

"Brilliant CX ideas within companies are already there, but often never given a chance to be heard."
– **Mitch Belsley**

359

"In customer experience, the little things matter as much, if not more, than the big things."
– **Adrian Swinscoe**

360

"Never ever underestimate the influence you have on customers."
– Lee Cockerell

"Quite simply, without employees, you have no customer experience. Put the employee experience first."
– Annette Franz

362

"Every interaction with a customer is an opportunity to earn, or lose, their trust. The aggregate of these moments is your customer's experience which defines the relationship, your future opportunities, and their loyalty."
— **Ellie Wu**

"You'll make better decisions about your customers when you know what they do, how they think and how they feel when they are not interacting with your brand."
– **Sandra Thompson**

364

"If you're competitor–focused, you have to wait until there is a competitor doing something. Being customer–focused allows you to be more pioneering."
– **Jeff Bezos**

365

"No one is ever not in an experience."
– James Dodkins

My name is James Dodkins, I used to be an actual, real–life, legitimate, award–winning rockstar…but now I'm not.

Now, I'm a 'Customer Experience Rockstar'.

You might know me from my musical CX keynote 'Rules For Rockstars', my weekly news show 'This Week In CX' or my super cool CX workshops…alternatively you may have never heard of me before.

Either way, if you're looking for an unforgettable CX keynote or a transformative CX workshop please keep me in mind, take a look at my videos at www.jamesdodkins.com and get in touch at james@jamesdodkins.com.

Printed in Great Britain
by Amazon